A WINNING SKILLS BOOK

You Can Be Beautiful!

Joy Berry

Illustrated by Bartholomew

Joy Berry Enterprises

Copyright © Joy Berry, 2022
Originally Published 2013

All rights are reserved.

No part of this book can be duplicated or used without the prior written permission of the copyright owner, except for the use of brief quotations from the book.

For inquiries or permission requests contact the publisher.

Published by Joy Berry Enterprises
www.joyberryenterprises.com

Joy Berry
Enterprises

You can be beautiful if you understand
- the definition of classic beauty,
- the definition of cultural beauty,
- the definition of genuine beauty,
- advantages and disadvantages of each kind of beauty,
- eight guidelines for becoming genuinely beautiful, and
- eight tips for enhancing genuine beauty.

THE DEFINITION OF CLASSIC BEAUTY

Beauty is the quality of being pleasing to look at. Beautiful people are attractive. It is pleasing to look at them.

There are many ways people define beauty.

Some people feel that beauty is based on standard measurements applied to the human face and body. The more a person's face and body conform to these standards, the more beautiful the person is considered to be. This kind of beauty is often called *classic beauty*.

The illustration gives some measurements for the classically beautiful face.

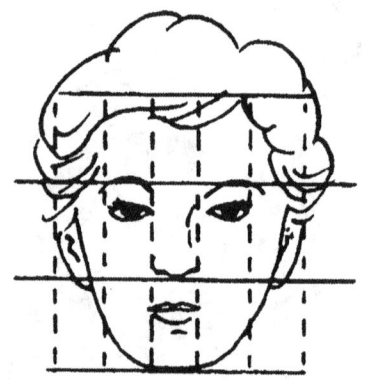

When horizontal lines are drawn at the forehead hairline, the eyebrows, the base of the nose, and the bottom of the chin, all three sections should be equally spaced.

The width of the face should be five times the width of one eye.

Using the eye as the basic measurement, the face should be proportioned in this way.

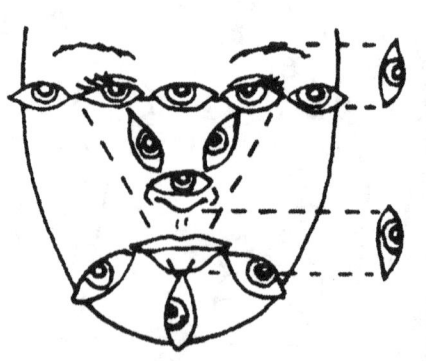

THE DEFINITION OF CLASSIC BEAUTY

Here are some more measurements for the classically beautiful face.

#1, 2, and 3 should line up in the male profile.

The ear should be positioned in the middle section and should be as long as the distance from the top of the eyes to the bottom of the nose.

#1, 2, and 3 should line up in the female profile.

The angle of the nose should be 125°.

THE DEFINITION OF CLASSIC BEAUTY

Here are some of the measurements for the classically beautiful male body.

Using the head as a basis for measurement, the male body should be 8 heads tall and the shoulders should be 2 horizontal heads wide.

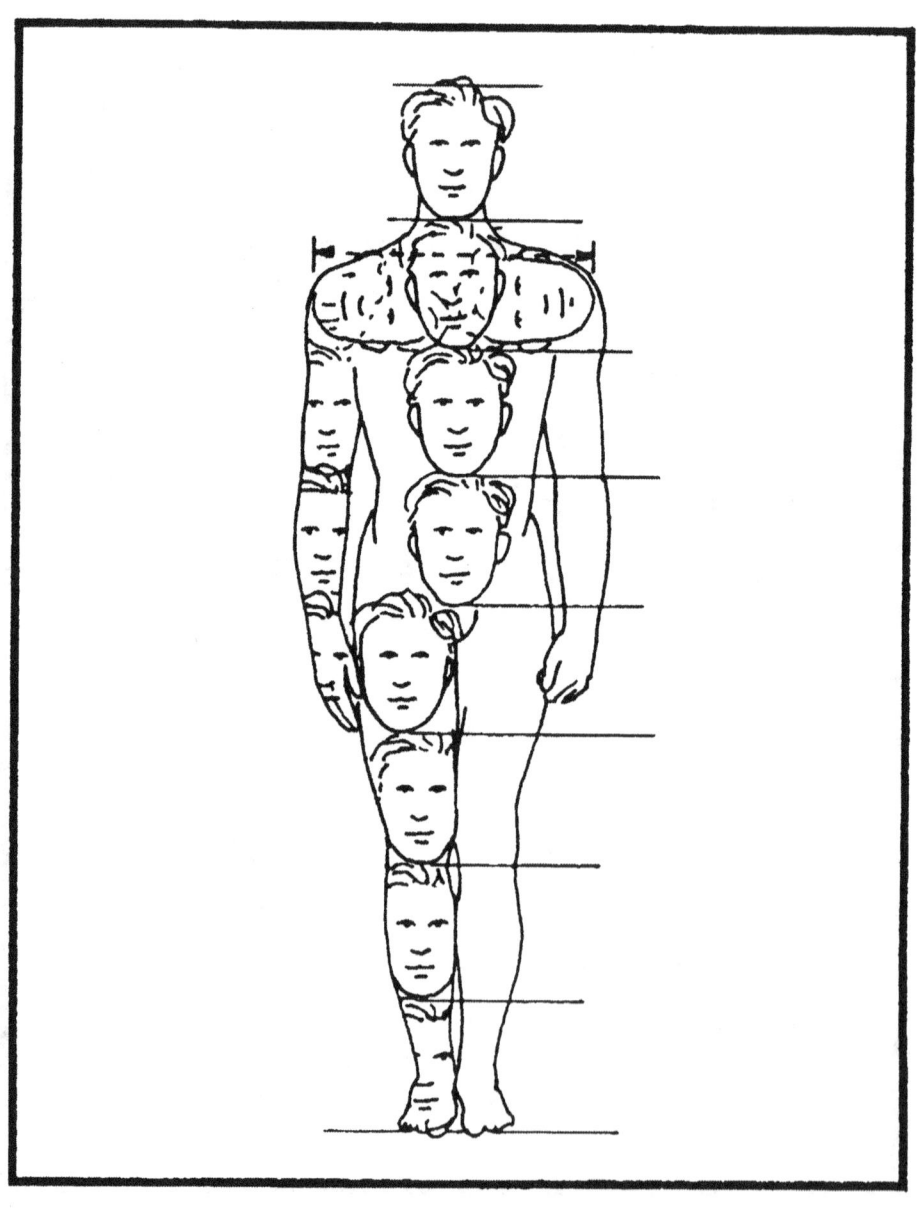

THE DEFINITION OF CLASSIC BEAUTY

Here are some of the measurements for the classically beautiful female body.

Using the head as a basis for measurement, the female body should be 7 1/2 heads tall and the shoulders should be 2 vertical heads wide.

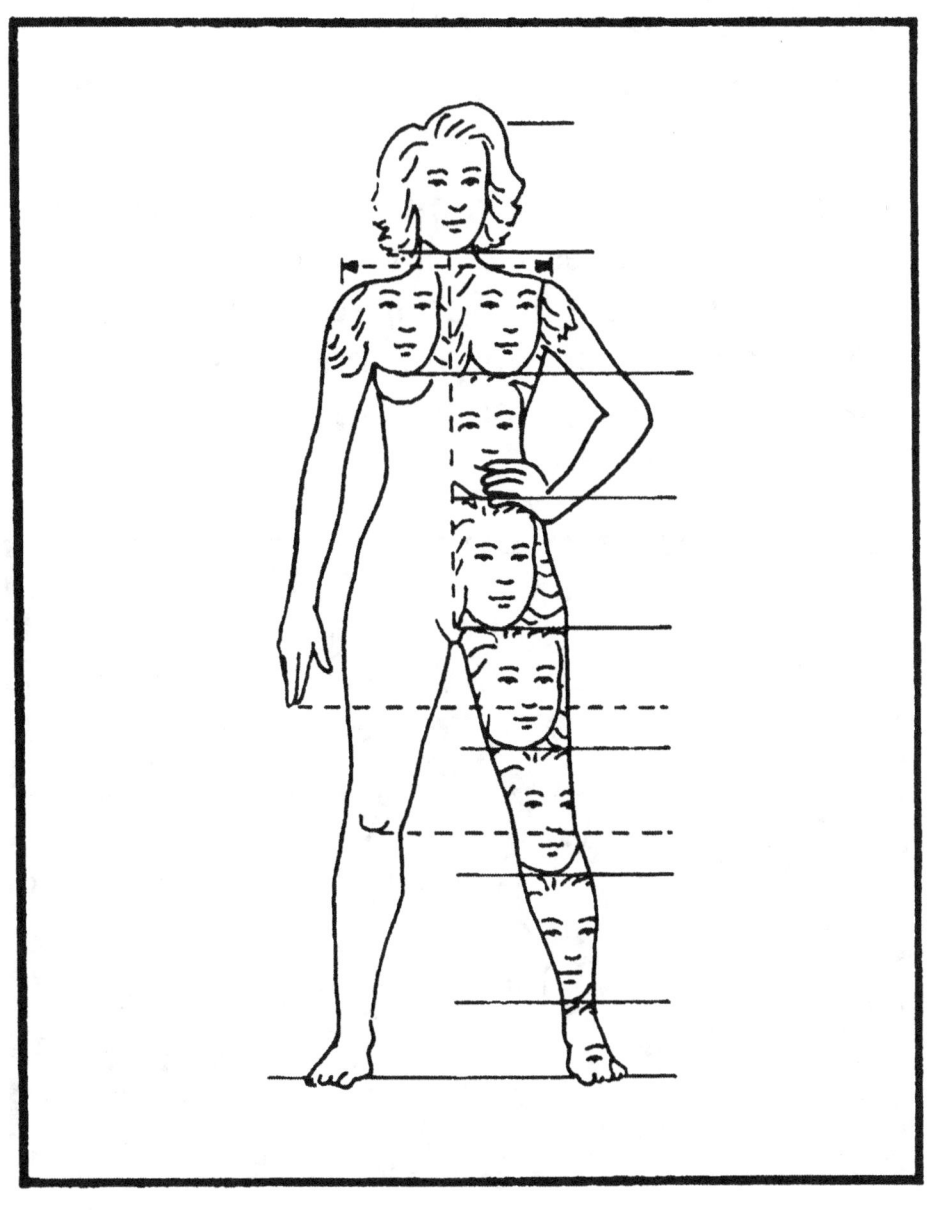

THE DEFINITION OF CULTURAL BEAUTY

Some people feel that beauty is based on standards established by a culture or society. These standards reflect the thinking, values, and major events of the culture or society, and they change as the culture or society changes. The more a person's physical appearance conforms to the standards set by the culture or society, the more beautiful the person is considered to be.

This kind of beauty is often called **cultural beauty**.

For example, in some past societies, wealthy people had access to an unlimited food supply and were not required to toil in the sun. The heavier, white-skinned bodies of these people became the standard of beauty for those societies.

In some societies, poor people tended to be heavy because their diet consisted mainly of high-caloric foods. Being heavy became associated with being poor and having to live on such foods. As a result, being extremely thin became the standard of beauty among wealthy people in those societies.

THE DEFINITION OF CULTURAL BEAUTY

In some societies, wealthy people who were concerned about their health and who had leisure time to invest in keeping fit became involved with health spas, clubs, and fitness programs. They also participated in outdoor athletic activities. As a result, the muscular, suntanned body became the standard of beauty for those societies.

THE DEFINITION OF CULTURAL BEAUTY

The hairstyles, make-up, and clothing that help set the standards for cultural beauty are determined by the people who make up the society. These standards frequently change over time.

THE DEFINITION OF GENUINE BEAUTY

Some people think that beauty is a combination or outer and inner qualities that every person can develop and maintain.

This kind of beauty is often called **genuine beauty**. The qualities that make up genuine beauty are often called **inner** and **outer** beauty.

Outer beauty is based on maintaining an attractive physical appearance. The healthier and more well groomed a person's body, the more outer beauty the person is considered to have.

Outer beauty creates a "glow" (a pleasant expression) that can complement any kind of beauty.

THE DEFINITION OF GENUINE BEAUTY — 13

Inner beauty is based on a person's basic attitudes and actions. The more positive the person's attitudes and actions, the more inner beauty the person is considered to have.

Inner beauty translates into a personality that is genuine, caring, and giving. Inner beauty creates a "radiance" that shines through a person's physical appearance, no matter how "beautiful" or "homely."

BEAUTY: ADVANTAGES AND DISADVANTAGES

As with everything, each kind of beauty has advantages and disadvantages.

Classic and cultural beauty both have some advantages.

If you have classic or cultural beauty, you might
- possess a positive self-image,
- attract attention,
- garner admiration and compliments,
- discover open doors to job offers and other opportunities,
- have increased opportunities for relationships with the opposite sex, and
- enjoy dressing up.

Classic and cultural beauty both also have some disadvantages.

If you have classic or cultural beauty, other people might
- be jealous of you,
- assume that you are conceited,
- feel inferior and thus avoid being around you, or
- be preoccupied with you physical beauty and ignore other good qualities about you.

If you classic or cultural beauty, you might
- rely so much on your appearance that you fail to develop other, more important attributes and abilities,
- wonder whether people like you merely for your beauty and for no other reason, or
- fear that you life will be ruined if your beauty should be lost.

Classic and cultural beauty can also
- attract attention when you don't want it,
- attract attention from people you don't want to associate with, or
- diminish with the passing of time.

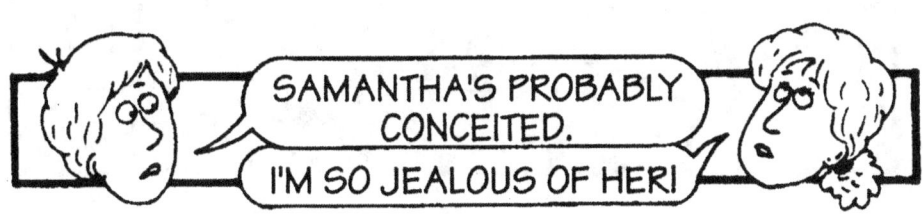

BEAUTY: ADVANTAGES AND DISADVANTAGES

Genuine beauty, like classic or cultural beauty, has advantages.

If you have genuine beauty, other people usually
- like you,
- respect you,
- trust you, and
- want to be around you.

Having genuine beauty can
- enhance your self-image,
- raise your level of self-confidence,
- help you develop and maintain positive relationships with others, and
- help you develop and maintain long-term relationships with the opposite sex.

Genuine beauty is something you can develop and maintain no matter what happens to you or around you. Also, genuine beauty is something that is enhanced as you get older.

BEAUTY: ADVANTAGES AND DISADVANTAGES

Genuine beauty also has some disadvantages.
- Genuine beauty is not always immediately recognizable. Sometimes it takes time for genuine beauty to be discovered and acknowledged.
- Because genuine beauty must be developed and maintained, it requires
  - personal discipline,
  - time, and
  - effort.

BEAUTY: ADVANTAGES AND DISADVANTAGES

Classic and cultural beauty are mostly based on characteristics that are present at birth. People have little control over whether they possess classic or cultural beauty.

Genuine beauty is mostly based on characteristics developed during a lifetime. People have a great deal of control over whether they possess genuine beauty.

This means that no matter what kind of face and body a person is born to have, he or she has the potential to develop genuine beauty.

People with classic or cultural beauty can lose their attractiveness with time or when trends change. However, people with genuine beauty are always attractive.

No matter how beautiful people look on the outside, if they are not beautiful on the inside, they will not remain attractive to others. This is what is meant by saying, "Physical beauty is only skin-deep."

Another saying is, "Beauty is as beauty does." This means that whether a person is beautiful depends more on the person's actions than on his or her looks.

Because genuine beauty is the only kind of beauty that you have control over and the only kind that is long-lasting, it is best to invest your time and energy in developing and preserving genuine beauty.

EIGHT GUIDELINES FOR BECOMING GENUINELY BEAUTIFUL

Here are eight guidelines that can help you develop genuine beauty.

The first four guidelines have to do with inner beauty.

Guideline #1: People who are genuinely beautiful love and respect themselves.

They realize that they are valuable because they are unique and have a special purpose in life.

Genuinely beautiful people respect and take care of themselves physically, mentally, emotionally, and spiritually.

Guideline #2: People who are genuinely beautiful love and respect other people.

They realize that every person is valuable because he or she is unique and has a special purpose in life. Genuinely beautiful people live by the golden rule: "Treat other people the way you want to be treated."

This means that they truly care about others and are sensitive, kind, giving, and fair. They are also understanding and forgiving whenever necessary.

Guideline #3: People who are genuinely beautiful are positive in their thoughts and actions.

They are people who generate and focus on positive rather than on negative thoughts. They find and affirm the good things that are present in every person and situation.

Genuinely beautiful people strive to replace negativity with positive thoughts and actions. They work diligently in acceptable ways to bring about constructive change in the things that need to be changed.

Guideline #4: People who are genuinely beautiful are honest.

They are not deceitful. They do not pretend to be something they are not. They do not hurt others by lying to them.

Genuinely beautiful people can be trusted because they say what they mean in a kind way and keep whatever promises they have made.

People who have inner beauty have a radiance that can make them extremely attractive. This radiance shines from the inside out.

Outer beauty can either detract from or enhance the radiance generated by inner beauty. For example, if you wrap a beautiful gift in dirty old newspaper, the gift might not appear to be as valuable as it would had you wrapped it attractively.

Although outer beauty should not be the focus of anyone's life, it needs to be developed so that it can complement a person's inner beauty rather than detract from it.

The next four guidelines have to do with outer beauty.

Guideline #5: People who are genuinely beautiful are healthy.

They eat a well-balanced diet that includes
- carbohydrates provided by such foods as whole grains, fruit, and vegetables;
- protein provided by such foods as fish, poultry, lean meat, milk, cheese, eggs, and certain grains, beans, and peas;
- unsaturated fats provided by such foods as fish, beans, corn, nuts, and olive oil;
- fiber provided by such foods as raw fruits, vegetables, and whole-grain bread and cereals;
- vitamins provided by such foods as milk, eggs, whole-grain foods, yeast, fruits, vegetables, lean meat, fish, and nuts; and minerals provided by such foods as milk, cheese, eggs, lean meat, fish, dried fruits, and vegetables (especially green leafy ones).

A well-balanced diet is one that includes the following foods every day:
- 2 fruits (one should be a citrus fruit, such as an orange)
- 2 vegetables (one should be a dark green or deep yellow)
- 3 or more cups of skim milk (or servings of other foods high in calcium, such as green leafy vegetables)
- 2 or more servings of cheese, eggs, lean meat, fish, poultry, beans, or peas.
- 4 or more servings of whole-grain foods.

Healthy people **have good eating habits**. They avoid eating too much of certain foods, such as sugar, salt, and fat, that can be harmful to the body. These foods include "junk food," such as soda, candy, pastries, cookies, cake, and sugary cereals.

Artificial sweeteners, and foods that contain them, must also be avoided because they cause a craving for sweets.

Note: People who have a difficult time avoiding sweet foods might lack important minerals. Certain mineral deficiencies cause a craving for sweets. If you crave sweets, you might want to talk to your doctor or nutritionist.

Healthy people
- sit down whenever they eat and avoid "eating on the run;"
- eat to nourish their bodies, **not** to reward themselves or to make themselves feel better;
- have their breakfast, lunch, dinner and snack at approximately the same time every day;
- eat only when they are hungry;
- eat slowly;
- chew their food thoroughly before swallowing it; and
- stop eating when they feel full, even if some food remains on the plate.

Healthy people **drink plenty of water**. They drink several glassfuls every day. They also drink more water on warm days and whenever they are especially active.

Healthy people **get plenty of fresh air and sunshine**.

To make sure their bodies are getting enough fresh air and sunshine, they work and play outside as often as possible. They also wear sunscreen, a protective cream that helps prevent sunburn. Too much exposure to the sun can cause skin cancer.

Guideline #6: People who are genuinely beautiful are physically fit.

They exercise regularly and include aerobic exercise as part of their exercise program.

To be effective, aerobic exercise should
- increase the breathing and heart rate,
- continue for at least 20 to 30 minutes,
- include both "warm-up" and "cool-down" (stretching) exercises, and
- be done at least three or four times a week.

Some activities that provide aerobic exercise include aerobic dancing, running, jogging, fast walking, uphill hiking, jumping rope, bicycling (at least 12 miles per hour), full-court basketball, rowing, swimming, and cross-country skiing.

"Stop and go" activities, such as tennis, handball, racquetball, football, baseball, and downhill skiing, might not provide aerobic exercise but still help you develop a fit and healthy body.

Physically fit people **get plenty of rest and sleep**.

They make sure their bodies are getting enough rest and sleep by
- taking time during the day to rest whenever they feel tired, and
- sleeping at least eight hours every night.

Guideline #7: Genuinely beautiful people are clean and well groomed.

They
- shower or bathe everyday,
- clean around their eyes everyday,
- clean out their ears and nose everyday, and
- clean their faces at least twice a day.

People who are clean and well groomed also
- shampoo and rinse their hair at least three times a week (every day if possible),
- brush their teeth at least twice a day (preferably three times a day), and
- clean their nails every day and manicure them at least every other week.

Guideline #8: People who are genuinely beautiful maintain good posture.

They make sure that when they are standing, these parts of the body line up.

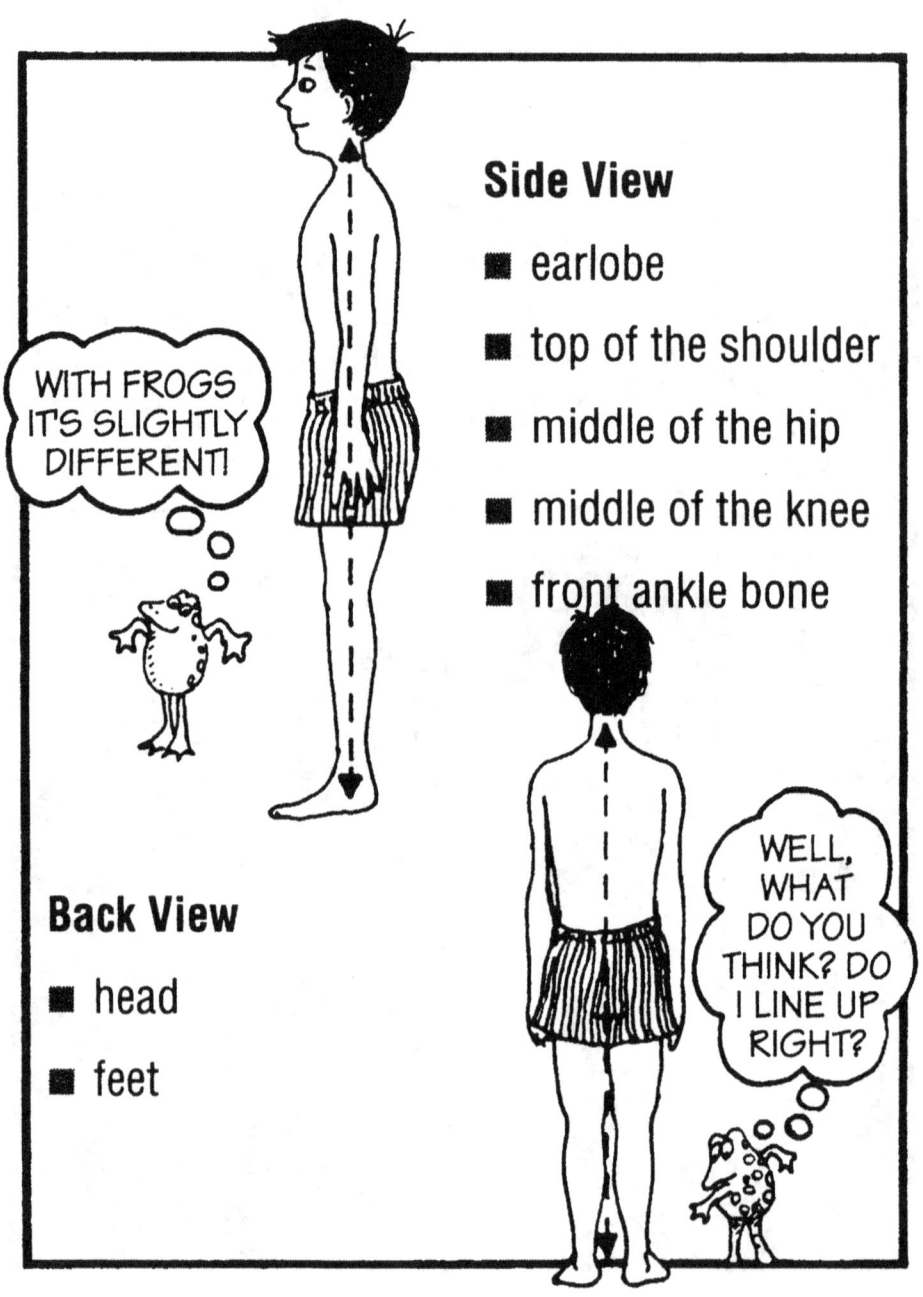

Side View
- earlobe
- top of the shoulder
- middle of the hip
- middle of the knee
- front ankle bone

Back View
- head
- feet

People with good posture sit correctly in a chair by placing the small of their back against the back of the chair and keeping the feet flat on the floor or crossed at the ankle.

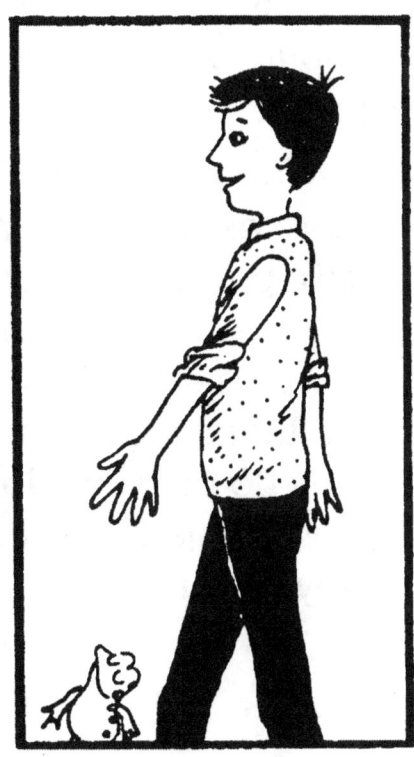

People with good posture "walk tall." This means they walk as if they were being pulled up by the hair on top of their heads. They walk with the natural curve of the back, and head, neck, and spine in alignment, with the shoulders down.

They point their feet straight ahead or very slightly outward.

In addition to following the eight guidelines, you can practice eight tips to enhance your genuine beauty.

Tip #1: Accentuate your best physical features and overlook your worst ones.

Decide what you think are the best features about your head and body and then focus on these.

Decide what you think are your worst features and then try to overlook them. Being unhappy about features you cannot change is a waste of time and energy. It might help if you remember that most human beings, no matter how beautiful they are, have features they do not like. No one is perfect, and very few people are completely satisfied with the way they look.

Tip #2: Choose a simple hairstyle that makes you feel beautiful.

Do not choose your hairstyle on the basis of another person's hairstyle or opinions. Only you can determine what makes you feel beautiful.

Your hairstyle should be as natural and as simple as possible. Spending too much time on your hair uses up valuable time that could be spent on other, more important things.

When choosing a hairstyle, consider whether your own basic profile is straight, concave, or convex. The right hairstyle can enhance your profile and minimize features such as a large nose or a protruding chin.

Tip #3: If you wear make-up, use as little as possible.

Make-up should be as simple as possible.

Heavy make-up can detract from your inner and outer beauty.

A good rule to follow is this: You are wearing too much make-up if it is noticeable or becomes a focus of attention.

Tip #4: Wear colors that enhance your natural coloring.

Try on many different colors to see which ones look best. Colors that match your hair and eyes will almost always look good on you.

If your coloring is:	Try to wear these colors:
Pale to pink skin/ blonde hair	Beige (if your skin is not too pale), violet, mauve, navy, blue, green, peach
Dark skin/blonde to light-brown hair	Burnt orange and rust, red, gold bright blue, beige, olive green brown, peach
Dark or olive skin/ red hair	Brown, apricot, beige, light brown, mauve, purple, navy, bright blue, rust, deep brown
Fair skin/brown to black hair	Blue, white, yellow, gold, red, mauve, purple, navy, bright blue, pastel blue, gray, brown
Dark skin\brown to black hair	Bright colors, such as turquoise, bright green, raspberry, purple, pink

EIGHT STEPS FOR ENHANCING GENUINE BEAUTY

Tip #5: Wear clothes that make you look and feel beautiful.

The size and shape of your body are very important in choosing clothes.

If you are tall, you will probably look best in
- plaids,
- prints,
- full skirts (for girls),
- soft ruffled blouses (for girls),
- pleated pants,
- contrasting colors,
- horizontal lines, and
- bulky seaters.

You might want to avoid
- severely tailored clothes,
- one-color outfits, and
- vertical lines.

If you are short, you will probably look best in
- one-color outfits or coordinated outfits,
- clothes with small (rather than large) details,
- short vests and jackets (for girls),
- pleated skirts (for girls), and
- vertical lines or stitching.

You might want to avoid
- hems that are longer than a few inches below the knee (for girls),
- hems that are shorter than a few inches above the knee (for girls), and
- horizontal lines.

If you are slender you will probably look best in

- the layered look,
- plaids,
- prints,
- full skirts (for girls),
- bulky sweaters,
- soft ruffled blouse (for girls),
- pleated pants,
- contrasting colors, and
- horizontal lines.

You might want to avoid

- severely tailored clothes,
- one-color outfits, and
- vertical lines.

If you are heavy, you will probably look best in
- darker colors,
- flared skirt (for girls),
- tailored pants,
- long or three-quarter length sleeves, and
- simple styles.

You might want to avoid
- bright colors,
- large plaids,
- large prints,
- shiny fabrics,
- extra frills (for girls),
- pleated skirts (for girls),
- pleated pants, and
- clothes that fit tightly.

Tip #8: Avoid becoming obsessed with your outer beauty.

Outer beauty is like a picture frame that surrounds a beautiful work of art. The frame is necessary to hold and display the artwork. However, the frame is not more important than the artwork and should not receive more time and attention than the work of art.

Although outer beauty is important, the focus needs to be on developing your inner beauty.

Thinking of yourself as beautiful is essential to being beautiful. Thinking you are beautiful causes you to **act** as if you are beautiful, and acting as if you are beautiful helps you to **become** beautiful.

Thoughts originate in the mind, so it is important to keep you mind focused on thoughts that help enhance your inner beauty.

Make a list of all your qualities of inner and outer beauty. If necessary, ask for help from family and friends. Add to the list every time you discover another aspect of your beauty.

Study the list at least once a day until you begin thinking of yourself as a beautiful person.

CONCLUSION

A genuinely beautiful person is one who
- loves and respects himself or herself,
- loves and respects others,
- is positive,
- is genuinely caring and giving,
- is healthy,
- is physically fit,
- is clean and well groomed, and
- maintains good posture.

The potential to be genuinely beautiful is something every person has, including you!

www.ingramcontent.com/pod-product-compliance
Lightning Source LLC
Chambersburg PA
CBHW081408070526
44583CB00020B/2724